W9-AKB-761

SERGEY BRIN

BY SARA GREEN

FREEPORT MEMORIAL LIBRARY

BELLWETHER MEDIA • MINNEAPOLIS, MN

Jump into the cockpit and take flight with Pilot books. Your journey will take you on high-energy adventures as you learn about all that is wild, weird, fascinating, and fun!

This edition first published in 2015 by Bellwether Media, Inc.

No part of this publication may be reproduced in whole or in part without written permission of the publisher. For information regarding permission, write to Bellwether Media, Inc., Attention: Permissions Department, 5357 Penn Avenue South, Minneapolis, MN 55419.

Library of Congress Cataloging-in-Publication Data

Green, Sara, 1964- author.
  Sergey Brin / by Sara Green.
      pages cm. – (Pilot. Tech Icons)
  Summary: "Engaging images accompany information about Sergey Brin. The combination of high-interest subject matter and narrative text is intended for students in grades 3 through 7"– Provided by publisher.
  Audience: Ages 7-12.
  Includes bibliographical references and index.
  ISBN 978-1-60014-993-1 (hardcover : alk. paper)
  1. Brin, Sergey, 1973–Juvenile literature. 2. Google (Firm)–Juvenile literature. 3. Internet industry–United States–Biography–Juvenile literature. 4. Web search engines–History–Juvenile literature. I. Title.
  TK5105.885.G66G66 2014
  338.7'6102504092–dc23
                          2014011917

Printed in the United States of America, North Mankato, MN.

TABLE OF CONTENTS

CHAPTER 1
WHO IS SERGEY BRIN?   4

CHAPTER 2
AN AMERICAN EDUCATION   6

CHAPTER 3
**A MATH AND
COMPUTER GENIUS**   10

CHAPTER 4
GOOGLE INC.   14

CHAPTER 5
CONTRIBUTING TO SOCIETY   18

LIFE TIMELINE   20

GLOSSARY   22

TO LEARN MORE   23

INDEX   24

WHO IS SERGEY BRIN?

In 1996, Sergey Brin forever changed the way we find information. That year, he helped launch Google, the most popular **search engine** in the world. Google made Internet searches easier than ever before. Its popularity made Sergey very rich. In 2014, he was worth more than $31 billion! Sergey continues to push the limits with Google. He hopes to make the world a better place through free and open information.

Sergey was born into a Jewish family on August 21, 1973. He was an only child for many years. His brother, Sam, was born in 1987. Sergey spent the first years of his life in Moscow, Russia. At that time, the country was part of the **Soviet Union**. The Soviet government had harsh rules. Some were unfair to Jews. Sergey's father, Michael, did not agree with the government. He wanted a better life for his family in the United States.

ICON BIO

Name: Sergey Mikhaylovich Brin

Birthday: August 21, 1973

Hometown: Moscow, Russia

Marital status: Married Anne Wojcicki in 2007; separated in 2013

Children: One boy and one girl

Hobbies/ Interests: Yoga, sports cars, roller hockey, gymnastics

CHAPTER 2

AN AMERICAN EDUCATION

The Brin family was in luck. In 1979, the Soviet government gave them permission to leave the country. Sergey's parents were overjoyed! The Brins moved to the United States and settled in Maryland. Michael taught math at the University of Maryland. His mother, Eugenia, was a scientist.

Sergey went to elementary school in Adelphi, Maryland. The first year was difficult. Sergey's English was poor, and he spoke with a strong Russian accent. The other kids could not understand him. Sergey felt bashful and struggled to make friends. Luckily, Sergey was very bright. He enjoyed puzzles, maps, and math games. The teachers encouraged him to learn at his own pace. He pursued his interests in math and science. The teachers soon saw that Sergey had outstanding math skills. Young Sergey was also interested in computers. His father bought him one when he was 9 years old.

A PROUD HERITAGE

Sergey attended Hebrew school as a child. He studied Jewish culture and Hebrew, the traditional language of Jews. When he was 11 years old, Sergey visited the Jewish country Israel.

Sergey's intelligence continued to impress his teachers through middle school and high school. He thrived in most subjects, but math was his favorite. He raced through the work for gifted students easily. He even corrected his math teachers when they made mistakes.

Sergey also enjoyed listening to his father discuss math problems with other professors. Once, he solved a problem that had stumped his father's college students!

By the time he was 15, Sergey was bored with his high school classes. He began taking classes at the University of Maryland. Sergey soon earned a year's worth of college credits there. After his junior year, he left high school. He entered the University of Maryland as a full-time student.

CHAPTER 3
A MATH AND COMPUTER GENIUS

Sergey **majored** in math and computer science at the university. After only three years of study, he graduated near the top of his class. Sergey's next goal was to earn a PhD like his father. His hard work helped him win a **scholarship**. This paid for many of the costs of school. Sergey chose to attend Stanford University in Palo Alto, California. There he pursued a PhD in computer science.

At Stanford, Sergey's main interest was **data mining**. He used computers to gather information and look for patterns. Sergey was a brilliant student. He passed all of the exams for his PhD in a few months. Students often take years to pass these tests. Sergey then had time for other activities. He enjoyed rollerblading, swimming, and gymnastics. He even learned to fly on a **trapeze**.

Sergey is part owner of a Boeing 767 jet. It includes a private cabin for Sergey, complete with a king-sized bed.

11

"As we go forward, I hope we're going to continue to use technology to make really big differences in how people live and work."
— Sergey Brin

In the spring of 1995, Sergey met a computer science student named Larry Page. They did not get along at first, but over time they became friends. At that time, the **web** was fairly new. People were still learning how to use it. Sergey and Larry began to work on ways to collect information on the web. They studied how web sites were connected. Sergey liked mining all the information on the web. It was a challenge and a thrill.

Sergey and Larry worked day and night on their project. They invented a program that improved **query** results. It listed pages based on their popularity. This had never been done before. Sergey and Larry called their program PageRank. They used it to create a new search engine. They named it Google based on the mathematical term **googol**. It represented the vast amount of information on the web.

A POPULAR TERM

The word *google* is so commonly used that it is now in the dictionary. It means "to use Google to search for information on the Internet."

CHAPTER 4

GOOGLE INC.

The first version of Google went on the Stanford University web site in 1996. It was popular right away. But Sergey and Larry had a problem. The university's computer system could not handle all the traffic. Sergey and Larry decided to put their PhDs on hold and start a company.

In 1998, the two men moved to Menlo Park, California. There, they launched Google Inc. from a friend's garage. Sergey served as president of the new company. Larry was the **CEO**. The company was an instant success. Users loved how fast the search engine worked. It provided better information than any other search engine. Sergey and Larry's company grew quickly. Soon, the garage was too small for the company. In 1999, Google moved to several buildings in Mountain View, California. Sergey and Larry called the campus the "Googleplex."

MILLIONS OF SEARCHES

In 2013, people performed about 6 million Google searches every day.

"We want Google to be the third half of your brain."
— Sergey Brin

Over time, Google created other services in addition to the search engine. People use Google's email and chat programs to keep in touch with family and friends. Many rely on Google's maps for directions.

Today, Sergey manages a part of the company called Google X. There, scientists work to solve problems with technology. Some projects are top secret. Others, such as the self-driving car and Google Glass, have been shared with the public. The self-driving car is being tested on roads in several states. Glass is a computer that fits on users like a pair of glasses. Scientists are also working on a special contact lens. It measures blood sugar levels in the tears of people with **diabetes**. Another Google X project uses balloons to improve Internet access to people who live in the countryside. Sergey continues to seek ways that Google can help people. His ideas have brought the company great success. In 2014, Google was worth almost $400 billion!

AN OUTER SPACE VACATION

In 2008, Sergey put money into a company called Space Adventures. $5 million reserved him a seat on a future flight to outer space.

CHAPTER 5
CONTRIBUTING TO SOCIETY

Sergey is not only a successful **entrepreneur**. He is also a **philanthropist** who believes in giving back. In 2005, he and Larry Page started a **foundation** called Google.org. Each year, it donates millions of dollars to support education, wildlife, and children. It also seeks to reduce **poverty** around the world. Sergey also **co-founded** The Brin Wojcicki Foundation. It gives millions of dollars to helping people and funding medical research.

In 2009, Sergey donated $1 million to the Hebrew **Immigrant** Aid Society. This group helped his family move to the United States in 1979. Sergey has also donated millions of dollars to Parkinson's disease research. Parkinson's disease is a brain disorder that affects walking, speaking, and moving. Sergey's mother has this disease. Someday Sergey might get it, too. There is currently no cure. However, thanks to Sergey's generous donations and dedication to open information, scientists may find a life-saving solution.

RESUMÉ

Education

1993-1998: Stanford University, M.S. Computer Science (Palo Alto, California)

1990-1993: University of Maryland, B.S. Mathematics and Computer Science (College Park, Maryland)

1987-1990: Eleanor Roosevelt High School (Greenbelt, Maryland)

Work Experience

2011-present: Director of Special Projects, Google X

2001-2011: President of Technology, Google

1998-2001: President of Google

Community Service/Philanthropy

2013: Donated $32 million to the Michael J. Fox Foundation

2012: Donated $222.9 million to the Brin Wojcicki Foundation

2005: Established Google.org foundation; committed nearly $1 billion to charities around the world

LIFE TIMELINE

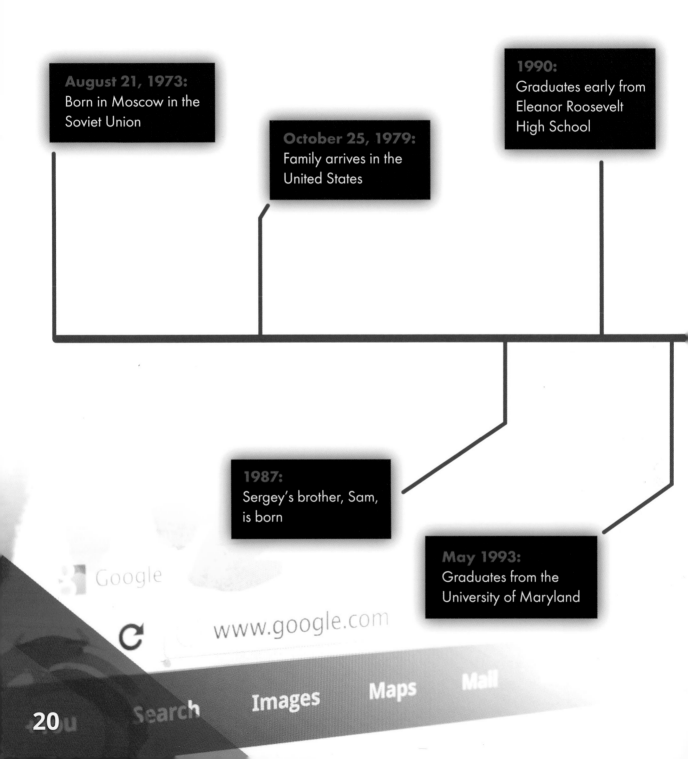

August 21, 1973:
Born in Moscow in the Soviet Union

October 25, 1979:
Family arrives in the United States

1990:
Graduates early from Eleanor Roosevelt High School

1987:
Sergey's brother, Sam, is born

May 1993:
Graduates from the University of Maryland

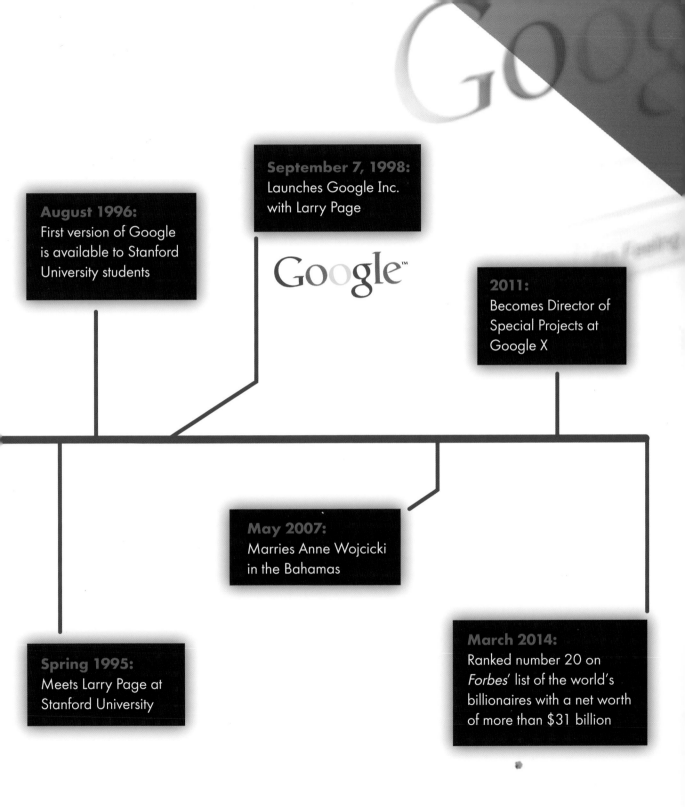

August 1996:
First version of Google is available to Stanford University students

September 7, 1998:
Launches Google Inc. with Larry Page

Google™

2011:
Becomes Director of Special Projects at Google X

May 2007:
Marries Anne Wojcicki in the Bahamas

Spring 1995:
Meets Larry Page at Stanford University

March 2014:
Ranked number 20 on *Forbes'* list of the world's billionaires with a net worth of more than $31 billion

21

GLOSSARY

CEO—Chief Executive Officer; the CEO is the highest-ranking person in a company.

co-founded—founded a company with one or more people

data mining—using computers to collect information and then look for meaningful patterns hidden within it

diabetes—a disease that causes high levels of sugar to be in the blood; diabetes can lead to blindness, nerve damage, and kidney failure.

entrepreneur—a person who starts a business

foundation—an organization that provides funds to other charitable organizations

googol—the mathematical term for a one followed by 100 zeros, or 10^{100}

immigrant—a person who leaves one country to live in another country

majored—studied for a specific degree

philanthropist—a person who gives time and money to help others

poverty—the state of being poor

query—a request for information that is made using a search engine

scholarship—an award that gives a student money to pay for college

search engine—a program that collects and organizes information from the Internet

Soviet Union—a large country in eastern Europe and western Asia that broke up in 1991

trapeze—a swing from which circus performers hang

web—an information system on the Internet that allows documents to be linked to other documents

TO LEARN MORE

AT THE LIBRARY

Flammang, James M. *Larry Page and Sergey Brin*. Ann Arbor, Mich.:
Cherry Lake Pub., 2008.

Green, Sara. *Larry Page*. Minneapolis, Minn.: Bellwether Media, 2015.

Sutherland, Adam. *The Story of Google*. New York, N.Y.: Rosen
Central, 2012.

ON THE WEB

Learning more about Sergey Brin
is as easy as 1, 2, 3.

1. Go to www.factsurfer.com.

2. Enter "Sergey Brin" into the search box.

3. Click the "Surf" button and you
    will see a list of related web sites.

With factsurfer.com, finding more information
is just a click away.

INDEX

Brin Wojcicki Foundation, 18

childhood, 4, 6, 7, 9

education, 6, 7, 9, 10, 14

family, 4, 6, 10, 19

Google, 4, 13, 14, 16

Google.org, 18

Google Glass, 16

Google X, 16

Googleplex, 14

Hebrew Immigrant Aid Society, 19

hobbies, 6, 10, 17

Internet, 4, 16

Jewish, 4, 7

Page, Larry, 13, 14, 18

PageRank, 13

philanthropy, 18, 19

self-driving car, 16

services, 16

Soviet Union, 4, 6

Stanford University, 10, 14

timeline, 20-21

United States, 4, 6, 19

University of Maryland, 6, 9, 10

worth, 4, 16